Gunnar Hering Lectures

Volume 2

Edited by
Maria A. Stassinopoulou

The volumes of this series are peer-reviewed.

Efi Avdela

When Juvenile Delinquency Became an International Post-War Concern

The United Nations, the Council of Europe and the Place of Greece

V&R unipress
Vienna University Press

Bibliographic information published by the Deutsche Nationalbibliothek
The Deutsche Nationalbibliothek lists this publication in the Deutsche
Nationalbibliografie; detailed bibliographic data are available online:
http://dnb.d-nb.de.

**Publications of Vienna University Press
are published by V&R unipress GmbH.**

Sponsored by the Austrian Society of Modern Greek Studies, the Department for
Cultural Affairs of the City of Vienna (MA 7), the Department of Byzantine and
Modern Greek Studies and the Faculty of Historical and Cultural Studies
at the University of Vienna.

Cover image: *Die reale Abstraktion*, 2011, silkscreen on paper,
68 x 90 cm, © Stefania Strouza
Printed and bound by CPI books GmbH, Birkstraße 10, 25917 Leck, Germany.
Printed in the EU.

Vandenhoeck & Ruprecht Verlage | www.vandenhoeck-ruprecht-verlage.com

ISSN 2625-7092
ISBN 978-3-8471-0941-9

Preface

This essay is based on a contribution to the Gunnar Hering Lectures, presented at the Department of Byzantine and Modern Greek Studies, University of Vienna, on 25 April 2017. I am grateful to Professor Maria Stassinopoulou for inviting me and to Professor Oliver Rathkolb for agreeing to comment on my lecture. It is a great honor to give this prestigious lecture named after an important historian. I did not have the privilege of knowing or meeting Gunnar Hering and our research paths only crossed occasionally. But because of its rigor and depth, and especially its wide scope, his work remains exemplary.

Introduction

> Delinquency is not the name of an illness, nor is there one simple specific psychological category for all delinquents and for them alone. Yet still today, doctors, magistrates, and teachers seem to be dominated, though often almost unconsciously, by a belief in a specific psycho-biological delinquent type.[1]

This is how Dr. Lucien Bovet, the author of a study composed in 1950 on behalf of the World Health Organization as a contribution to the United Nations programme for the prevention of crime and the treatment of offenders, summarized the predicament of this

---

[1] L. Bovet, *Psychiatric Aspects of Juvenile Delinquency*, World Health Organization, Palais des Nations, Geneva, 1951, p. 8.

new post-war public concern. Indeed, juvenile delinquency generated strong anxieties in the years following the end of the Second World War on both sides of an increasingly divided Europe and in many other parts of the world. As it gained public attention, the question of dealing with the purportedly widespread "antisocial" behavior of young people also gave rise to developing struggles over expertise. A forensic psychiatrist, head of the medical educational office of the Department of Justice and State Police of Vaud, at Lausanne, Dr. Bovet repeatedly claimed in his report that psychiatrists were better placed to explain and confront juvenile delinquency than physicians, jurists, or educators.

This essay examines how the intensive activity around the issue of juvenile delinquency of the new international bodies which emerged after the end of the Second World War, such as the World Health Organization, the various services of the United Nations and the Council of Europe, internationalized the anxieties generated in the fifties and sixties by its purported increase in Europe and beyond. It argues that in the post-war conditions, juvenile delinquency and its prevention became an opportune social issue of wide concern, apt to foster international collaboration while consolidating political and professional hierarchies in a troubled world order. Greece, a regular member-state of all these organizations from their start, participated systematically in the conferences organized on the subject of juvenile delinquency and contributed data to the reports, surveys and recommendations that were produced. However, it will argue that in order to ensure international legitimacy, Greek authorities presented abroad an embellished picture of the initiatives and measures undertaken for the prevention and containment of juvenile delinquency. At the same time, at home, strong moralism and juridical formalism dominated both official and unofficial approaches to the issue.

The essay first outlines briefly the terms under which juvenile delinquency became an international public issue during the first decades after the war, and the ambiguities surrounding its understanding and treatment. The second part focuses on the reports from the main international conferences on juvenile delinquency organized by the United Nations, the World Health Organization, UNESCO, and the Council of Europe during the 1950s and 1960s, and their successive conclusions and guidelines. This material, compiled according to data provided by state members, transnationalized the issue and—in spite of the repeatedly formulated reservations—fostered comparisons and the crystallization of differences and commonalities, among other issues concerning appropriate expertise. At the same time, insisting on the need for scientific approaches to the issue, the international activity around it homogenized and depoliticized it according to the priorities of the dominant—usually Western European—countries.

The third part sketches how the issue of juvenile delinquency was dealt with in Greece during the post-war period, both at the level of discourse and at the level of public policies, and underlines the prevailing moralism. The final part examines the place of Greece in the above international organizations. While its representatives systematically attended conferences and contributed to surveys, everything indicates that their presence was rather perfunctory. Greek authorities constantly provided information that created an embellished image of the existing preventive measures while they insisted that the culturally dominant model of strong family ties made this country more immune than others to the excesses of juvenile delinquency. Motivated by a nationalist urge to improve the country's image abroad at a time of acute social and political divisions at home, the relevant discourse sidestepped the strong moralism and the juridical formalism that dominated the field concerning juvenile delinquency at the national level.

Transnational anxieties over juvenile delinquency: a post-war issue

That juvenile delinquency became a matter of public concern in the post-war period is well documented.[2]

---

[2] To give but a few examples: for the USA: J. Gilbert, *A Cycle of Outrage. America's Reaction to the Juvenile Delinquent in the 1950s*, Oxford, 1986; L. Passerini, "La jeunesse comme métaphore du changement social. Deux débats sur les jeunes: L'Italie fasciste, l'Amérique des années 1950", in G. Levi and J.-C. Schmitt (eds), *Histoire des jeunes en Occident*, vol. 2: *L'époque contemporaine*, Paris, 1996, pp. 339–408. For Britain: L. Jackson (with A. Bartie), *Policing Youth: Britain 1945–70*, Manchester, 2014; M. Jarvis, *Conservative Governments, Morality and Social Change in Affluent Britain, 1957–64*, Manchester, 2005; A. Wills, "Delinquency, Masculinity and Citizenship in England 1950–1970", *Past & Present* 187, 2005, pp. 157–185. For Sweden: R. Nilsson, "Creating the Swedish Juvenile Delinquent: Criminal Policy, Science and Institutionalization c. 1930–1970", *Scandinavian Journal of History* 34/4, 2009, pp. 354–375. For Holland: M. Komen, "Dangerous Children: Juvenile Delinquency and Judicial Intervention in the Netherlands, 1960–1995", *Crime, Law & Social Change* 37, 2002, pp. 379–401. For Italy: S. Piccone Stella, "'Rebels without a Cause': Male Youth in Italy around 1960", *History Workshop Journal* 38, 1994, pp. 157–178. For the Soviet Union: M. Edele, "Strange Young Men in Stalin's Moscow: The Birth and Life of the Stiliagi, 1945–1953", *Jahrbücher für Geschichte Osteuropas* 50/1, 2002, pp. 37–61 and J. Fürst, *Stalin's Last Generation. Soviet Post-War Youth and the Emergence of Mature Socialism*, Oxford, 2010. For Hun-

Historical research has shown that in many countries —in Europe and beyond—youth became a source of growing anxiety. Journalists, opinion makers, and politicians shared the widespread belief that youth demonstrated—to an extent unknown before—one form or other of antisocial or unlawful behavior and that the numbers of juvenile offenders were constantly increasing. Adolescent males were considered the main source of concern. They were accused not only of committing different kinds of illicit acts, such as theft and aggression, but also of entertaining unconventional cultural practices—such as loud music, sartorial preferences, or love of speed. Specialists did not always agree in their interpretations of this disquieting development, but they all related it to a wide range of factors, the special weight of which they appreciated differently: disrupted family relations and unacceptable permissiveness of parents, but also physical and psychological consequences of poverty and poor living conditions in urban areas, inadequate state care and education, and the new forms of youth entertainment.

The public concerns about juvenile delinquency were of course not new in the years after the end of the

gary: S. Horváth, "Patchwork Identities and Folk Devils: Youth Subcultures and Gangs in Socialist Hungary", *Social History* 34/2, 2009, pp. 163–183. For Greece: E. Avdela, "'Corrupting and Uncontrollable Activities': Moral Panic about Youth in Post-Civil-War Greece", *Journal of Contemporary History* 43/1, 2008, pp. 25–44. For Israel: M. Ajzenstadt, "Reactions to Juvenile Delinquency in Israel, 1950–1970: A Social Narrative", *The Journal of Policy History* 17/4, 2005, pp. 404–425. For a more comparative approach: H. Ellis (ed.), *Juvenile Delinquency and the Limits of Western Influence, 1850–2000*, London, 2014. The next few paragraphs draw from my "Youth 'in Moral Danger': (Re)conceptualizing Delinquency in Post-Civil-War Greece", *Social History* 42/1, 2017, pp. 73–74. I thank the editors for their permission.

Second World War. In fact the issue constitutes a notable early example of transnational diffusion of ideas and expertise. Since the late nineteenth century the successive international penal congresses dedicated to the "criminal child" had contributed to the elaboration of the concept of "delinquency" and to the formation of a wide network of transnational European experts, characterized recently as an "epistemic community in the making."[3] With the end of the First World War the anxieties about its impact on orphaned or impoverished children and youth contributed to the collaboration between the League of Nations with the International Penal and Penitentiary Commission and the Save the Children International Union in a series of conferences aiming at outlining the problem of juvenile delinquency and at formulating future policies.[4]

In the post Second World War period, however, the public anxieties over juvenile delinquency became more widespread than they had ever been before. As the existing historiography indicates, they mobilized everywhere a multitude of national and international public and private agents—administrators, governments, the Church, wel-

---

[3] S. Kott, "Une 'communauté épistémique' du social ? Experts de l'OIT et internationalisation des politiques sociales dans l'entre-deux-guerres", Genèses 71/2, 2008, pp. 26–46. For the concept of "epistemic community" see P. Haas, "Introduction: Epistemic Communities and International Policy", *International Organization* 46/1, 1992, pp. 1–35.

[4] J. Droux, "L'internationalisation de la protection de l'enfance : acteurs, concurrences et projets transnationaux (1900–1925)", *Critique internationale* 52/3, 2011, pp. 17–33; M.-S. Dupont-Bouchat, "Du tourisme pénitentiaire à 'l'Internationale des philanthropes'. La création d'un réseau pour la protection de l'enfance à travers les congrès internationaux (1840–1914)", *Paedagogica Historica: International Journal of the History of Education* 38/2-3, 2002, pp. 533–563.

fare institutions, the press—as well as different experts—psychologists, psychiatrists, educators, social workers, physicians, and jurists. While the power relations between groups of experts differed in each country according to the academic traditions and the leverage each discipline had on state authorities, the general trend was the move from penal to "psy" approaches. The same anxieties also galvanized the new international bodies established after the end of the Second World War, such as the World Health Organization, the various services of the United Nations, and the Council of Europe. Their intensive activity around the issue of juvenile delinquency generated repeated reports, conferences, surveys, and recommendations, some of which are analysed below.

The "transnational discourse" on juvenile delinquency,[5] that is, the mass of national and international writing and the transnational diffusion of ideas about this public concern and the policies for its prevention and containment, wavered during this period between two distinctive features: claims of scientific status and strong moralism. A third feature was the discrepancy, ever more frequently admitted, between the intensity of public anxieties and the diffuse phenomenon that generated them. Because it was so difficult to delineate with some precision the extent of the "phenomenon," and given the insistence of public anxieties, preventive measures became the focus of national and international debates and interventions. With the legacies of the traumatic past still vivid, in the midst of a process of reconstruction that

---

[5] H. Ellis, "Editor's Introduction: Juvenile Delinquency, Modernity, and the State", *Social Justice* 38/4, 2011, p. 4; K. Bertrams and S. Kott, "Actions sociales transnationales", *Genèses* 71/2, 2008, pp. 2–3.

triggered unpredictable changes in all realms of private and public life, in the acute political polarization of the Cold War context, dealing with juvenile delinquency became a metonym for taming the unknown and restoring authority in the public and the private domains.

The very term "juvenile delinquency" was full of ambiguities. The need to distinguish between "criminality" and "delinquency" with respect to the unruly behavior of minors became ever more accepted among jurists from the end of the nineteenth century.[6] In the following period, the development of the concept of adolescence, the constitution of criminology and psychology as academic disciplines, and the establishment of social work as a profession, reinforced this idea. It was crystallized by the subsequent establishment of juvenile justice mechanisms and their corresponding institutions and agencies, public and private. By the post-war period the term "juvenile delinquency" predominated in the field and in most countries prevention took precedence over repression;[7] however not everywhere nor to the same degree.

For instance, in the Greek case the term "juvenile delinquency" was never used during the period in question. Official texts, scholarly publications and the press saw

---

[6] C. Leonards, "Border Crossings: Care and the 'Criminal Child' in Nineteenth Century European Penal Congresses", in P. Cox and H. Shore (eds), *Becoming Delinquent: European Youth, 1650–1950*, Aldershot, 2002, pp. 105–121.

[7] The historiography on these issues is immense. For general overviews: A. Binder, A. Geis, D.D. Bruce, *Juvenile Delinquency. Historical, Cultural, Legal Perspectives*, Cincinnati, 1997; J. Muncie, *Youth and Crime. A Critical Introduction*, London, 1999. See also in Greek my *"Νέοι εν κινδύνω". Επιτήρηση, αναμόρφωση και δικαιοσύνη ανηλίκων μετά τον πόλεμο* ['Youth in Danger'. Surveillance, Reformation and Juvenile Justice after the War], Athens, 2013.

young offenders, unruly youth, and minors in "moral danger" as parts of the same social phenomenon—"child and youth criminality" [*paidiki kai neaniki egklimatikotita—παιδική και νεανική εγκληματικότητα*]. In the post-Civil-War context the issue of "child and youth criminality" found socially and ideologically fertile ground, and was at the centre of public debates.[8] The need to protect minors from the "moral dangers" of both the negative legacies of the bloody 1940s and the rapid transformations of the present haunted the public, the political parties, the Church, state officials, and the press as well as jurists and social scientists, and it developed into a moral panic about youth—in the sense that Stanley Cohen has given to the term.[9] While it lasted, diverse and contingent acts were treated as part and parcel of a single social phenomenon, consistently identified as "underage criminality."[10] This homogenization was reinforced by the limited development of new expertise in related issues. Psychiatrists, psychologists, social workers, and juvenile probation officers were nascent experts, with as yet negligible public leverage. The limited development of the social sciences, the restricted influence of the "psy" sciences, and the recent (in 1940) establishment of the juvenile justice mechanism meant that the project of reforming unruly youth and the technologies of power that were employed remained for decades the prerogative of tradi-

---

[8] For the Greek Civil War (1946–1949) see: D. H. Close, *The Origins of the Greek Civil War,* London, 1993 and T. D. Sfikas and P. Carabott (eds), *The Greek Civil War. Essays on a Conflict of Exceptionalism and Silences*, Aldershot, 2004.

[9] S. Cohen, *Folk Devils and Moral Panics: The Creation of the Mods and Rockers*, London, 1972.

[10] Avdela, "'Corrupting and Uncontrollable Activities'", and Avdela, "Youth in 'Moral Danger'."

tional forces: jurists, the Church, journalists, and politicians. Amidst the political configuration of the post-Civil-War years, as a consequence, moralism prevailed in lay and scholarly discourse and in the various interventions and policies.

Debating juvenile delinquency in the international fora: experts and others

Public concerns about the purported increase in juvenile delinquency found listening ears in the new "transnational network of specialists," as Akira Iriye has termed the institutions and committees created after the war in response to the foundation of the United Nations and other supra-national bodies.[11] In the middle of growing international divisions fed either by the Cold War or decolonization, these bodies aimed at widening the scope of international relations far beyond diplomacy. Therefore they showed immediate interest in issues referring to the various social ills with which member-states were confronted. It was believed that concerted efforts around such issues could promote international cooperation amidst increasing polarization, both political and economic. Crime and its prevention, an issue of both public and social order, were given central place.

---

[11] A. Iriye, "The Making of a Transnational World", in A. Iriye (ed.), *Global Interdependence. The World after 1945*, Cambridge, Mass., London, 2014, pp. 722–723. From the vast literature on the history of the United Nations, see, indicatively, R. Jolly, L. Emmerij, T.G. Weiss, *UN Ideas that Changed the World*, Bloomington & Indianapolis, 2009; M. Mazower, *No Enchanted Palace. The End of Empire and the Ideological Origins of the United Nations*, Princeton, 2009.

It is in this context that in 1948 the secretary general of the United Nations convened a committee of experts to study and propose an international programme for the prevention of crime and related necessary actions. The Commission considered that juvenile delinquency was a matter of particular importance and should be given priority. Accepting that the issue concerned medical and psychiatric problems, its study was assigned to the World Health Organization—newly founded as a UN specialized agency.[12] The mission was given to Dr. Lucien Bovet, whose report was based on research in several European countries and the USA. Published in 1951, *Psychiatric Aspects of Juvenile Delinquency* soon became a classic reference.[13]

Bovet's dispassionate discourse on an issue that had already generated high passions was an eloquent defence of the need for new scientific approaches. First of all, he repeatedly emphasized the difficulties in circumscribing "juvenile delinquency": not only did its legal definition vary from country to country, but also—as the quote cited at the beginning shows—deeply rooted convictions often dominated in the treatment of juvenile offenders. Since it was impossible to demonstrate objectively the validity of these convictions, Bovet asserted that "[i]t must be rare for decisions with serious coercive consequences to be taken with so little supporting evidence as in the case of juvenile delinquency."[14] Therefore, anxie-

---

[12] A. Iriye, *Global Community. The Role of International Organizations in the Making of the Contemporary World, Los Angeles*, London, 2002, pp. 42–43.

[13] Bovet, *Psychiatric Aspects of Juvenile Delinquency.* See also Leonards, "Border Crossings."

[14] Bovet, *Psychiatric Aspects of Juvenile Delinquency* , p. 10.

ties were exaggerated and much more research was urgently needed.

Even more, Bovet strongly objected to the term "juvenile delinquency." He considered it "legal and social in origin" and not scientific. He preferred the terms "social dis-adaptation or maladjustment," which did not necessarily equate to delinquency. At any rate, however understood, juvenile delinquency was for Bovet a "bio-psycho-social phenomenon," and its three constitutive dimensions should always be taken into equal account.[15] While he underlined the necessity of concerted efforts between a variety of experts for the study and treatment of juvenile delinquency, he repeatedly presented psychiatry not only as more clear-headed and effective in dealing with most aspects of the phenomenon under study but also more appropriate for overcoming the half-century long opposition between constitutive and sociological aetiologies. In his words:

> The psychiatrist, whose training is both biological and psychological, with his interest in social problems, and with the knowledge he should have of inter-human relationships, could play a useful part in co-ordinating the efforts of the different specialists in juvenile delinquency and in helping them to work together with mutual understanding.[16]

That competing bodies of knowledge came into conflict over claims to expertise in the field of juvenile delinquency during the post-war decades is well attested in recent studies. These conflicts concerned the control of this field, all the more politicized as it became a matter of

---

[15] *Ibid.*, pp. 12, 41.
[16] *Ibid.*, pp. 79, 81–82.

public concerns and policies. As Bradley, Logan and Shaw have already noted for Britain, concepts such as "childhood," but also "adolescence" and "juvenile delinquency," "became [s]ource[s] over which many formal agencies (such as social workers and psychiatrists) would battle for control throughout the 1950s and 1960s."[17]

Soon after Bovet's study, the United Nations institutionalized the committee of experts on the prevention of crime, by absorbing as consultant experts the previously autonomous inter-governmental International Penal and Penitentiary Committee, founded at the end of the nineteenth century.[18] In subsequent years, the UN Economic

---

[17] K. Bradley, A. Logan, S. Shaw, "Editorial: Youth and Crime: Centennial Reflections on the Children Act 1908", *Crimes and Misdemeanours* 3/2, 2009, p. 11 and J. Muncie and G. Hughes, "Modes of Youth Governance. Political Rationalities, Criminalization and Resistance", in J. Muncie, G. Hughes, E. McLaughlin (eds), *Youth Justice. Critical Readings*, London–New Delhi, 2002, pp. 1–18. For the point of view of the post-war police force, Commission internationale de police criminelle, *La Délinquance juvénile actuelle, ses formes et ses causes, ainsi que les mesures propres à sa prévention dans le cadre de la lutte internationale contre la criminalité. XVIe session, Paris, 9–12 June 1947. N° 15, Rapport du Dr M. Sebor*, Paris, 1947 (henceforth Police criminelle 1947); and of juvenile probation officers, Organisation des Nations Unies, *La Probation (Régime de la mise à l'épreuve) et les mesures analogue*, Melen, 1953.

[18] United Nations Archives and Records Management Section. Fonds International Penal and Penitentiary Commission (1872–1955) – AG-010, S-0915-0002-0003-00001-UC, IPCC Délégation de la Grèce, 1946–1950. According to A. L. Sayward, *The United Nations in International History*, London, Oxford, 2017, 76, 246; the International Penal Commission was founded in 1872, "following the First International Congress on the Prevention and Repression of Crime (London 1872), with the mandate to collect penitentiary statistics, encourage penal reform, and host future international conferences." Renamed as the International Penal and Penitentiary Commission (IPPC) in 1929, it hosted joint conferences with the League of Nations in 1925 (in Berlin), 1930 (London), and 1935 (Paris). During the Second World War it was dormant. After the war it was transferred to the United Nations in 1950, integrated into the Economic and Social Council (ECOSOC)

and Social Council, hosting the international Congresses on the Prevention of Crime and the Treatment of Offenders every five years, collaborated closely with other international bodies in common actions around juvenile delinquency, organizing conferences, publishing studies, and conducting surveys.[19] The discourse that they generated spoke volumes about both the above-mentioned conflicts over expertise and the consequent ambiguities surrounding the field, but also about the divergent public policies for its containment. First of all, the commonly accepted need to plan and implement effective prevention raised the thorny question of how to identify not so much juvenile offenders as those minors who were at risk of becoming offenders; in other words, how to prevent delinquency. Consequently, the distinction between the different categories of youth that generated public concern became increasingly blurred. While this was not something new, it was now recognized by those involved. For example, the 1960 report of the Council of Europe underlined the growing trend in many countries to assimilate "delinquent," "maladjusted" and "strayed" minors, or to focus on "pre-delinquent" children and on

---

in 1955 and undertook from 1955 the quinquennial UN Congresses on the Prevention of Crime and the Treatment of Offenders.

[19] The First Congress on Crime Prevention and Criminal Justice was held in Geneva in 1955, the Second in London in 1960, the Third in Stockholm in 1965, and the Fourth in Tokyo in 1970. See United Nations Office on Drugs and Crime, *United Nations Congresses on Crime Prevention and Criminal Justice 1955–2010. 55 years of achievement*, United Nations Information Service, Austria, 2010. Also, M. Lopez-Rey, "The First U. N. Congress on the Prevention of Crime and the Treatment of Offenders", *Journal of Criminal Law and Criminology* 47/5, 1957, pp. 526–538.

minors in "moral danger."[20] The fact that the boundaries between these categories became porous, fluid, and easily crossed was of great concern to both experts and authorities, since in essence it meant that all minors were considered as potentially in "moral danger" of becoming delinquent.

Some common themes come out of the relevant material, confirming the early remarks of Dr. Bovet. First, there was no consensus among member states about what constituted "juvenile delinquency"; second, nowhere were there adequate data documenting the exact size of the problem; third, systematic research on its causes was urgently needed; and fourth, not only had all preventive measures proved ineffective, but also it was impossible to access their results.[21] All the forms of discourse on juvenile delinquency produced in the decade following Bovet's report in the context of the various international bodies centred on these issues.

In 1959, a new study was recommended by the United Nations to reassess the situation of juvenile delinquency. It was again assigned to a forensic psychiatrist, Dr. T. S. Gibbens, Senior Lecturer at the Institute of Psychiatry of the University of London and consultant at the World Health Organization. Based on his own medical experience, recent literature and information obtained through visits in many countries, his report was submitted to the Second United Nations Congress on the Prevention of

---

[20] European Committee on Crime Problems, *Juvenile Delinquency in Post-War Europe,* Strasburg, 1960 (henceforth ECCP 1960), pp. 37–38.

[21] Cf. Police criminelle 1947; ECCP 1960, pp. 19, 60; European Committee on Crime Problems, *The Effectiveness of Current Programmes for the Prevention of Juvenile Delinquency,* Strasburg, 1963 (henceforth ECCP 1963), p. 89.

Crime and the Treatment of Offenders, held in London in June 1960.[22]

Gibbens followed closely the footsteps of his predecessor, Lucien Bovet. He noted the difficulties in defining juvenile delinquency, the growing rejection by the public of youthful behaviors that until recently were not considered delinquent, but also the new disturbing attitudes adopted by a growing number of young people. While he claimed again the "solid scientific base" of psychiatry and psychology compared to other expertise, he also underlined the increasing collaboration of experts in the study of juvenile delinquency. He maintained that the past conflicts between psychiatrists, criminologists, sociologists, and other experts had been replaced by a more peaceful co-existence and cooperation. In his view, social psychology constituted the new connecting tissue in the various approaches to juvenile delinquency, offering a more balanced consideration of the social, biological and

---

[22] It was published enriched with material from other reports presented at the same congress, namely the one of the Council of Europe. T. C. N. Gibbens, *New Forms of Juvenile Delinquency*, World Health Organization, Geneva, 1961, p. 7; also United Nations, Department of Economic and Social Affairs, *Second United Nations Congress for the Prevention of Crime and the Treatment of Delinquents*, London, August 1960, Special Police Departments for the Prevention of Juvenile Delinquency, Submitted by the International Criminal Police Organization— INTERPOL, General Secretariat, Paris, 1960 (henceforth UN, *Juvenile Delinquency*, 1960); United Nations, Department of Economic and Social Affairs, *Second United Nation Congress on the Prevention of Crime, UN Reports, New Forms of Juvenile Delinquency: Their Origin, Prevention and Treatment*, Paris 1960. Compare with the typed version of the report: World Health Organization, *New Forms of Juvenile Delinquency; Their Origin, Prevention and Treatment*, Report from the World Health Organization to the Second United Nations Congress on the Prevention of Crime and the Treatment of Offenders, London, 1960, LSE Library.

psychological dimensions of the phenomenon under study.[23]

Gibbens insisted that the existing statistical data did not confirm the strong anxieties expressed in many countries about the increase in juvenile delinquency. In his words: "One may perhaps ask whether the most significant change in the present situation is not the behavior of youths, but the fact that adults view it with more alarm than they used to."[24] In the same vein, Gibbens systematically undermined the most common arguments supporting this purported increase, such as that "antisocial" behavior derived from the growing economic autonomy of predominantly male working-class youths, from the spread of television, radio, cinema, and the press or from the trends for equality between the sexes. Adopting a pioneering perspective, Gibbens considered the new forms of offences committed by minors, such as car borrowing, shoplifting, or hooliganism, as indications of youth sub-cultures; therefore the related adult anxieties were exaggerated. In the same vein, he was critical of the practice in many countries of branding young people with specific names according to their dress-codes ("Teddy-boys, Halbstarke, blouson noirs, nozems, styliarski, etc."[25]) and holding them responsible for much of juvenile crime, including the most serious. He maintained that minor phenomena such as car borrowing, loud behavior in public or performance riots after rock'n'roll films or concerts should not be considered as forms of juvenile delinquency; they constituted "ritual-

---

[23] Gibbens, *New Forms of Juvenile Delinquency*, pp. 10–20.
[24] *Ibid*, p.21 for both quotes.
[25] Respectively, British, German, French, Dutch, and Soviet designations.

ized opportunities for free emotional expression." Real delinquency—he insisted—"arose, according to clinical experience, in much the same way today as yesterday, from serious deprivation and major disorders of family life."[26]

While Gibbens underlined the persistent lack of a scientifically valid way to evaluate preventive programmes, he insisted that the family, its cohesion, the affection and supervision provided by the parents were factors of paramount importance in preventing juvenile delinquency and that state intervention was necessary whenever these were lacking. He embraced therefore the model of the family as an "apolitical sanctuary"—to use the words of Tara Zahra—that had been promoted since the end of the war through international aid and especially through the influence of American experts.[27]

Bovet's and Gibbens' studies were written according to the academic standards of their time. They were based on primary data and secondary literature, they discussed the different positions on each aspect of the problem, and they offered balanced suggestions. At the same time, they were positioned, in the sense that they implicitly promoted the superior capacity of their own discipline in producing "objective" assessments of the subject under study. While the very circumstances under which their reports were commissioned testified to the political character that the issue of juvenile delinquency had acquired in the post-war period, Bovet and Gibbens contributed to "depoliticizing" it, in suggesting that public

---

[26] Gibbens, *New Forms of Juvenile Delinquency*, pp. 30, 33, 34.

[27] T. Zahra, *The Lost Children. Reconstructing Europe's Families after World War II*, Harvard, 2015.

concerns around it should be appeased. Writing in mitigated terms, they denied that juvenile delinquency was on the increase, they refused to relate it to youthful cultural practices, and they stressed the need to grant more autonomy to adolescents of both sexes. Thus they separated the public anxieties of the moment from what they considered "real" juvenile delinquency—the "socially maladjusted behavior" that derived from "serious" social disadvantage and "major" disturbed family relations, from inequality, poverty, and repression.[28] Approaching juvenile delinquency as a physical, psychological, and social "disorder," they were primarily interested in "scientifically" understanding what was at stake with the alarm over "antisocial" youth, a condition of any prevention. Their reasoning could not be further from the legal and juridical approaches that predominated in several countries, notably in Greece.

The material from the successive conferences organized during the 1960s by the World Health Organization, UNESCO, and the Council of Europe, usually in cooperation, was more diversified and contradictory than the studies of the two psychiatrists: proceedings, reports, and surveys recorded the positions of each member-state on a variety of issues and at the same time delineated the power relations between international instances, countries, and forms of expertise.[29] What is relevant here are

[28] For an analysis of how the turn to 'psy' perspectives of juvenile delinquency and the problem family in the post-war period contributed in promoting 'governable subjects', see N. Rose, *Governing the Soul. The Shaping of the Private Self*, London–New York, 1999.

[29] For the most relevant among many publications, see Bovet, *Psychiatric Aspects of Juvenile Delinquency*; ECCP 1960; UN, *Juvenile Delinquency*, 1960; Gibbens, *New Forms of Juvenile Delinquency*; ECCP 1963; W. C. Kvaraceus, *La Délinquance juvénile, problème du monde modern*, UNESCO,

23

the quinquennial international congresses of the United Nations on the Prevention of Crime and the Treatment of Offenders or the surveys of the European Committee on Crime Problems (CDPC), set up by the exclusively Western Council of Europe in 1958 in order to oversee and coordinate activities in the field of crime prevention and crime control.[30]

Let us pause for a while on these last surveys, which were organized twice, in 1958 and again in 1962. Aiming at gathering information about the extent of juvenile delinquency and the existing preventive programmes, they collected responses to a common questionnaire from a limited number of member-states (all belonging to the Western bloc), twelve and thirteen respectively. International administrators and government representatives collaborated in composing the two reports. Because they conveyed widespread convictions in many member-states and were not scientific texts, these reports contained certain remarks that would have been unthinkable in the Bovet and Gibbens studies. For example, the 1957 survey put forward the correlation between juvenile delinquency and the birth-rate of "less intelligent, less adaptable, less adequate and also less educated members of the population"; it also referred to studies maintaining "that considerable psychological damage can be done" by the increasing "habit of many young mothers of

Paris, 1964; United Nations, Department of Economic and Social Affairs, *Third United Nations Congress on the Prevention of Crime and the Treatment of Offenders*, Stockholm, 9–18 August 1965, New York, 1967 (henceforth UN, *Prevention*, 1967).

[30] The Council of Europe was created in 1949 and remained a Western club until the fall of the Berlin Wall. See B. Wassenberg, *History of the Council of Europe*, Strasburg, 2013.

working while leaving their children to be looked after" by others.[31] These remarks, and others in similar vein, suggested that Bovet's concerns about the "rooted convictions" that still predominated in respect to juvenile delinquency remained valid many years later.

However, both reports underlined how impossible it was to verify the widespread belief in "an increase in the number of abnormal or specially difficult youngsters," as the material provided was inadequate and "extremely heterogeneous in character."[32] This is why only the 1958 survey—published in 1960—ventured a comparison; the 1962 one—published a year later, in 1963—only presented the individual responses of each member-state. In fact, even the 1958 survey could only record tendencies. Nine countries (Austria, France, the Federal Republic of Germany, Greece, Italy, Norway, Sweden, Turkey, and the United Kingdom) registered an increase in juvenile delinquency in the 1950s. Only in Belgium and Denmark did there appear to be a "reasonably persistent decrease," whereas the situation in the Netherlands was not clear. No convincing explanations could be provided for these trends, while comparisons were highly controversial since "the unit for measuring the incidence of delinquency" was not the same in each country.[33] The 1958 survey also showed that in many countries public concerns categorized as "anti-social" juvenile behavior related to consumption and the new forms of entertainment and sociality among the young, and it was admitted that often the press tended to homogenize and exaggerate the phe-

---

[31] ECCP 1960, pp. 11, 13.
[32] *Ibid*, pp. 10, 11.
[33] *Ibid*, pp. 10, 21, 24–25.

nomena. In addition, it confirmed that "the distinction in law between delinquent children and other[s] ["maladjusted, neglected, or in need of protection"] [...] is becoming blurred" in many countries. While this was more pronounced in Scandinavia, Belgium, and the Netherlands, penal methods became increasingly flexible for young offenders and non-penal methods were also promoted for "pre-delinquent" children in other countries.[34]

Finally, the 1958 report emphasized the need for all countries to keep solid comparable criminal statistics and to conduct complex and in-depth criminological research on juvenile delinquency. In spite of this recommendation, the following 1962 survey had little new to show.[35] Again the material obtained could not be compared.

Therefore, after so many years of concerted international efforts, not only could the exact extent of juvenile delinquency not be measured, but also its prevention proved to be a controversial issue: not only were there no comparable data as to the effects of prevention, but in addition there was no convincing system of evaluating preventive action while there were also "differences of opinion as to what constitute[d] a 'scientific evaluation'." This failure in prevention was repeatedly attested in a number of United Nations reports and proceedings. It was expressed in a UNESCO report of the same period in the most blatant terms: "There is no real evidence that youth work of any kind prevents delinquency."[36]

---

[34] *Ibid*, pp. 50, 56.

[35] ECCP 1963. The material gathered was presented to the United Nations European Seminar the same year. The collaboration between the Council of Europe and the United Nations on juvenile delinquency was constant throughout the 1960s.

[36] The quotes respectively in ECCP 1963, pp. 6, 8, 9, 11, 89.

This admission, dramatic in its simplicity, given the magnitude of forces and resources devoted since the end of the war to "youth work" as a means for preventing "antisocial" behavior in minors, marked at the same time the new priorities for deterring juvenile delinquency: emphasis on the family and its cohesion, family allowances to improve the living conditions of minors in poor households, more efforts for schooling, better understanding for youthful cultural practices, more welfare provision and less penal treatment of offenders. This is how the public anxieties about youth gone astray subsided in the 1960s even before the emergence of what became known as the "spirit of '68."[37] Juvenile delinquency ceased to be a public concern, let alone an international one, and became again an issue for experts, albeit different ones than in the past. It ceased to be a political issue.

Dealing with juvenile delinquency the Greek way: between penalization and morality

Let us now turn to Greece and sketch briefly the history of the very distinctive ways in which official and unofficial actors in this country undertook the treatment of juvenile offenders and youth "in moral danger."

The emergence of the juvenile justice mechanism in Greece was from the start related to politically troubled times. It was established during the Metaxas dictatorship in the late thirties and began operating in 1940, a few

---

[37] G.-R. Horn, *The Spirit of '68: Rebellion in Western Europe and North America, 1956–1976*, Oxford, 2007.

months before the country entered the war.[38] During the turbulent years that followed, the care of juvenile offenders became the prerogative of the Societies for the Protection of Minors and the initiatives of their volunteers. Apart from assisting the juvenile judge, they undertook mainly charitable activities for the minors under their protection, namely raising money, monitoring those who were released from reformatories and prisons, trying to find jobs and shelter for the most needy of them or distributing gifts on holy days to those still confined. Probation became more organized and professional when the Juvenile Probation Officers' Service was established in 1954, as an independent service attached to the juvenile court. Its staff, volunteer university graduates at first, became paid employees from 1958, recruited following a special examination and short-term training. The Royal Welfare Foundation—a controversial semi-private institution created by the Queen and funded by the state—undertook their expenses, until they became public servants in 1976, after the fall of the military junta.[39]

All matters related to the juvenile justice mechanism —the juvenile courts, the Juvenile Probation Officers' Service, as well as the host of voluntary or semi-official associations dedicated to the work on strayed youth— came under the Division of Juvenile Justice of the Minis-

---

[38] For the Metaxas dictatorship, see, among others, M. Petrakis, *The Metaxas Myth: Dictatorship and Propaganda in Greece*, London, 2006.

[39] For the Juvenile Probation Officers' Service see E. Avdela, "Between Voluntary Workers and Public Servants: Juvenile Probation Officers in Greece, 1954–1976", in A. Dialla and N. Maroniti (eds), *State, Economy, Society (19th–20th centuries). Essays in Honor of Emeritus Professor George B. Dertilis*, Athens, 2013, pp. 27–53.

try of Justice. These institutions had authority over every child and youngster between seven and twenty-one years of age that came to their attention—the minors of the period.[40] Under the supervision of the Ministry of Justice and the juvenile judge, the Juvenile Probation Officers' Service had three goals: to provide the juvenile judge with a thorough "report of social investigation" containing information about the "troublesome" minor or the minor "in moral danger," and about their family and community; to offer suggestions as to the measures necessary for their successful reformation; and to undertake the minor's social and moral "rehabilitation," by supervising their behavior and providing assistance, guidance, and support. The service covered two separate but interconnected areas of intervention: "prevention" and "control." The latter involved those who had, in one way or another, broken the law; they were usually accused of misdemeanours. The former concerned the minors considered to be "in moral danger," a slippery, fluid, and indefinite notion covering a range of "unacceptable" behavior from disobedience and flippancy to vagrancy, delinquency, and general "anti-sociality." Minors of both categories were mainly boys; girls never exceeded an average of ten to fifteen percent, more often in the category of those "in moral danger." Some were put in reformatory schools but the majority were assigned to juvenile probation officers. They all usually came from poor families, living in inadequate or even sordid conditions, suffering from unemployment and

---

[40] The Greek law distinguished three categories of legal penal minority, seven to twelve, thirteen to seventeen and eighteen to twenty-one. The JPOS dealt with all three categories.

without adequate supervision; in other words growing up in the harsh conditions that characterized the lives of the Greek post-Civil-War urban poor.[41]

All the agents for the moral reform of youth during the fifties and sixties considered the family to be crucial in shaping a minor's character and in keeping him or her away from "bad habits." They all celebrated the strength of Greek family ties, compared with other European countries. However, poverty, unemployment, and poor living conditions, which constituted the predicament for a large part of the Greek urban population in the 1950s and 1960s, were recognized as disrupting factors in a family's life and often drove minors into "moral danger" and the pitfalls of corruption. The juvenile probation officers could hardly contain their middle-class shock when time and again they depicted in detail in their reports the living conditions that prevailed in the shanty-towns surrounding Salonica and Athens where the supervised minors usually came from. However, they accepted that "anti-sociality" lurked mainly outside the confines of the family, in "bad company" and in "corrupting activities" that exerted a negative influence on the minor, the most persistent of which, for both boys and girls, was considered to be the cinema. "Anti-sociality" could also be the product of broken families, or cruel, indifferent or inadequate parents.

---

[41] E. Avdela, "Growing up in the 'Dangerous' Neighborhoods of Post-war Thessaloniki", in Evangelia Tressou, Soula Mitakidou, and Giota Karagianni (eds), *Roma Inclusion, International and Greek Experiences. Complexities of Inclusion*, Thessalonki, 2015, pp. 179–186 and Avdela, "Νέοι εν κινδύνω", whence ideas for the next few paragraphs have been drawn.

"Anti-social behavior" was presented in fixed gendered terms. For boys, it included stealing, truancy, insolence, loitering, avoiding school or a legal gainful occupation, frequenting billiard-houses, cinemas and bars, smoking, harassing women, and dressing improperly. Girls' "anti-sociality," on the other hand, was identified with "premature" sexuality, hanging out with boys, disobeying parents, going to parties and dressing in a "provocative" manner. Whether a girl was a virgin or not was an important indicator for assessing her prospects for "sound social behavior," and it was not rare for a juvenile probation officer to refer her to the forensic surgeon in order to establish her somatic condition. For both boys and girls the new forms of youth practices and norms of gendered behavior—what was often termed "modern line" and included rock music, casual clothes, youth magazines, cinema, and dancing parties—were considered imbued with "moral danger."

When in the 1950s the moral panic about youth developed in Greece, echoing the comparable international concerns through frequent press releases, the juvenile justice mechanism in its complex constitution of state, official, semi-official, and voluntary agents and services was being built up.[42] The two were related since the social phenomenon that stirred so many anxieties and interventions, the purported increase in "underage criminality," remained extremely difficult to measure and delineate: official penal and criminological statistics were not published prior to 1957, and even then the only information regarding juvenile delinquency that they con-

---

[42] Avdela, "'Corrupting and Uncontrollable Activities'", and Avdela, "Between Voluntary Workers and Public Servants."

tained referred to numbers of convictions in the juvenile courts. Although this was not a Greek particularity, it became more pronounced in this case because of the dominant place retained by the traditional agents of intervention, mainly state officials, jurists, various philanthropists, and the Church. Consequently, a strong moralism pervaded the discourses and policies on the issue, in a context of political authoritarianism and social inequality.

Systematic interventions were made through the concerted efforts of state authorities and private agents for more than a decade "to protect the moral and spiritual integrity of Greek children."[43] The Church, a myriad of associations for the protection of minors, the Ministry of Justice, jurists, and other professionals proclaimed repeatedly "the crusade to curtail the dangerous increase in child criminality [*paidiki egklimatikotita*, παιδική εγκληματικότητα]."[44] A classic example concerned the Societies for the Protection of Minors, founded in the 1940s in Athens, Piraeus and Thessaloniki, which in the following decades developed a wealth of public activities. Together with many different associations and a large number of individuals, volunteers as well as officials, often politically close to the government—sometimes also the Palace—and in cooperation with the Ministry of Justice, the Societies systematically organized public events aimed at sensitizing the public to the "anti-social

---

[43] *Καθημερινή* [*Daily*, henceforth *K*] 22.4.1952 and 24.11.1952. Avdela, "Youth 'in Moral Danger'."

[44] *K*, 16.11.1951. See also I. P. Papagerakis, *Οι μεταπολεμικοί ανήλικοι (Μελέτη κοινωνιολογική, ψυχολογική και παιδαγωγική)* [*Post-war Minors (A Sociological, Psychological and Pedagogic Study)*], Thessaloniki, 1956.

tendencies" of youth.[45] One was the "Week for the Strayed Child," organized in 1952, 1955 and 1958 with huge success, thanks to the support it received from most of the official institutions: including the Academy of Athens, the University of Athens, the Ministries of Justice, Education and Social Welfare, and the Archdiocese of Athens.[46] Another was the creation of Neighbourhood Committees for the Protection of Minors. Between 1958 and 1960 twelve such committees were created in different districts of Athens, in a "campaign" that was deemed "very successful." The aim of these committees was to prevent local children from "deviat[ing] from the right path"; they counted on the support of the local police departments, parishes as well as those inhabitants "distinguished for their morality and their social contribution."[47]

In the specific Greek context of the 1950s, characterized by diffuse political authoritarianism and intense political polarization, these initiatives were undertaken in the name of combating the "calamity of immorality" purportedly menacing Greek youth. In the 1950s moral-

---

[45] A. Kiriakopoulos, Alternative General Secretary of the National Federation of Greek Unions, speech in the auditorium of the Federation for the "Week of the Neglected Child" in 1958, mimeo, Archives of Union History, NFGU. For this week, see *Απογευματινή* [*Matinee*, henceforth *A*], 14 and 15.1.1958, pp. 1, 4 and 1, 5 respectively, and *Ελευθερία* [*Freedom*, henceforth *E*], pp. 10 and 16.1.1958, pp. 6 and 4 respectively. For the Youth and Spectacle Week, 25.11. and 2.12.1962, see *K*, 24.11.1962. For the Society of the Protection of Minors of Athens and its activities, see E. Avdela and D. Vassiliadou, "'Sauver l'enfant dévoyé': La Société pour la protection des mineurs d'Athènes après la guerre", *Revue d'histoire de l'enfance 'irrégulière'* 18, 2016, pp. 299–317.

[46] Avdela, "Youth 'in Moral Danger'", p. 82.

[47] *Ibid*, pp. 83–84 and Avdela and Vassiliadou, "Sauver l'enfant dévoyé."

ism was a crucial component not only of scholarly discourse, but also of governance. It constituted the ideological core of the conservative and nationalist Right in power, favouring the penalization of social and political behaviors and the repression of any kind of "deviation," even more so in respect to childhood and youth. Be that as it may, the above initiatives were also performed around social networks and political patronage. They constituted a social and political space of social provision that allowed individuals to build careers moving between volunteer associations and public institutions, on the condition that they were *"ethnikofrones"* (εθνικόφρονες, thinking nationally) and accepted the prevailing moralizing discourse.

In an attempt to coordinate the above related interventions, in 1953 the Ministry of Justice set up the Council for the Co-ordination of Juvenile Crime Prevention with the goal to achieve effective restraint "particularly with regard to the neutralisation of moral dangers for youth."[48] The Council operated for six years. Its con-

---

[48] *K*, 28.11.1951. *Official Minutes of the Parliamentary Sessions, 12 December 1952–10 June 1953*, Athens, 1953, pp. 280–284. The law establishing the Council provided that it was to be composed of representatives of all the official bodies—the Church, many Ministries, the army, professional associations, the Boy Scouts, and the National Foundation, created by King Paul; also by "one representative of each of the organisations, associations or unions functioning [in the area of the capital], which include in their institutive aims issues regarding the general protection and the elevation of the morals of the underage[d]." Law 2330/1953 "on the establishment by the General Direction of Penal Justice of the Ministry of Justice of the Coordinating Council for the Measures aimed at the Prevention and Control of Underage Criminality", *The Official Gazette* 69, 21 March 1953, pp. 455–456. The absence of professional experts such as psychologists and sociologists from the list is indicative of the non-existent development of Greek professional competence and expertise on issues of youth in Greece at the time.

siderable size, the constant lack of funding, but also the prevailing moralism and the dominance of the penal approach restricted considerably both its decisions and their effectiveness. Its main contribution was a number of recommendations.

The Ministry also adopted a number of preventive and repressive measures, such as age limits for access to various categories of films, special legislation concerning publications for children, provisions prohibiting the access of minors to nightclubs, state funding of several active associations for the protection of minors, and provisions for the organization of after-school activities "aimed at providing varied and appropriate forms of entertainment and distraction from corrupting, uncontrollable activities."[49] It also sustained private initiatives such as the morality test devised by the Professor of Psychology at the University of Athens, George Sakelariou. In 1954, Sakelariou founded the Organization for the Moral Armament of Youth, with the aim to contain the increase of "criminality" among Greek schoolchildren. For this purpose he devised a "bulletin of exercise in virtues," which he conceived as a system of moral armament against provocations. Adopted by the Ministry

---

No minutes of this Council have been found to date. Avdela, "Youth 'in Moral Danger'", pp. 82–83.

[49] Ministry of Justice, General Direction of Penal Justice, Direction of Administration and General Inspection, Section of Minors, *Σκοποί–προσπάθειαι–επιτεύξεις Συμβουλίου συντονισμού των μέτρων διά τους ανηλίκους. Στατιστική έρευνα της εγκληματικότητος. Διεθνείς υποδείξεις, Έκθεσις Γ. Απ. Κατωπόδη, Διευθυντού Διοικήσεως και Γενικής Επιθεωρήσεως Φυλακών και Καταστημάτων Ανηλίκων, υποβληθείσα προς τον Κον Υπουργόν της Δικαιοσύνης* [*Aims–Efforts–Achievements of the Council Coordinating the Measures for Minors. International Suggestions. Report by G. A. Katopodis, Director of Administration and General Inspection of Prisons and Institutions for Minors, submitted to the Minister of Justice*], Athens, 1956, p. 31.

of Education, the bulletin was distributed to schools all over the country.[50] However, no efforts were made to assess the effectiveness of these measures—which were all finally short lived—in the prevention of delinquency.

In fact, the only concrete measures were taken at the apex of the Greek moral panic about youth at the end of the 1950s. I refer here to the legislative decree 4000, "On the repression of some punishable acts" enacted in 1959, which increased penalties for misdemeanours committed by minors—injuries, insults or car thefts—when "from the way, the timing and the general circumstances [the specific act] testifies to particular insolence of the offender and provocation toward society."[51] This was preceded a few months earlier by the public ridicule of some minors accused of acting as "*teddiboides*" [*τεντιμπόηδες*], a term broadly used during the 1950s and 1960s that Hellenized the English term "teddy boys" and became the emblem of the moral "corruption" of youth. The punishment, initiated by the Police Director, included tonsure, tearing of the blue-jean revers, hanging of a tablet stating, "I am a *teddibois*" and procession in the streets of Athens. The unusual ritualized public punishment and the voting of the legislative decree were widely publi-

---

[50] V. Theodorou and V. Vassiloudi, "'Για να σφυρηλατήσουμε καλύτερους και πιο υπεύθυνους χαρακτήρες": Ψυχολογικά εργαλεία ηθικοποίησης της νεότητας στη μετεμφυλιακή Ελλάδα' ['In order to forge better and more responsible characters': Psychological tools for the moralisation of youth in post-Civil-War Greece], paper delivered at the Fourteenth Panhellenic Congress of Psychological Research, Alexandroupoli, 15–19.5.2013; My thanks to the authors. See also *K*, 13 March 1954, 6; Avdela, "Youth 'in Moral Danger'", p. 84.

[51] LD 4000/1959, "On the repression of some punishable acts and on the complement of the article 6 of the Code of Penal Procedure," 30 October 1959, *FEK* 23, 31 October 1959.

cized and operated as a catalyst. Together with the severe criticism of certain jurists of such extrajudicial practices, they produced a shift in the public attitude of state authorities and subsequently in public opinion. Henceforth, state officials as well as journalists would not tire of repeating—both at home and abroad—that Greek youth differed radically from the youth of other European countries, mainly because the Greek family maintained its disciplining role more than elsewhere.[52] This did not mean, however, that domestic policies and discourses on the issue changed: on the contrary, they remained persistently moralizing while juridical formalism continued to prevail throughout the sixties and early seventies.

Greece as part of the new international organizations: the patriotic duty of embellishment

As already mentioned, Greece, a regular member state of all the above international bodies from the start, participated systematically in the international conferences on juvenile delinquency and contributed data to the reports, surveys, and recommendations that were produced. However, the locally prevailing moralism and penal attitude toward "straying" youth was never expressed abroad.

The country's official participation in the international fora regarding juvenile justice had a long history. Greece had been a respected member of the International Penal Commission (IPU) since 1878. In the inter-war period its delegates were especially active, namely Panayiotis Skou-

---

[52] Avdela, "Corrupting and Uncontrollable Activities."

riotis, a high ranking civil servant of the Ministry of Justice, removed by the Metaxas dictatorship in 1936. In the 22nd Penal and Penitentiary International Congress of the International Penal and Penitentiary Commission (IPPC) in Rome, in 1940, three officials of the Ministry of Justice contributed reports on questions related to the treatment of juvenile offenders.[53] The upheavals of the 1940s—the war, the Occupation, and the subsequent Civil War—left their marks in the country's participation in the IPPC, dormant itself during the years 1939–1945.[54] But even after that date its presence remained rather shadowy. The dignitaries—a professor of criminology at the University of Athens and the General Director of Penal Justice at the Ministry of Justice—who were appointed as representatives of the Greek government seldom participated in any of the relevant collective activities, claiming financial reasons, while the country was late in paying its subscription by several years.[55] This seems to have remained so until the IPPC was absorbed by the UN in 1955 and the representatives of the mem-

---

[53] United Nations Archives and Records Management Section. Fonds International Penal and Penitentiary Commission (1872–1955) - AG-010, S-0915-0068-0005-00001 Part A UC: IPU, XXIIe Congrès pénal et pénitentiaire international de Rome, 1940 ; 1) Rapport présenté par M. Andreas Ch. Christodoulou, Directeur de l'Ecole d'éducation surveillée de Syros, Grèce; 2) Rapport présenté par M. le Dr. Themistocle G. Papaefstathiou, Directeur en chef de l'administration pénitentiaire, Athènes; 3) Rapport de M. G. Katopodis, Directeur de la prison-école 'Averoff' et de la Prison centrale des femmes (Athènes). Katopodis was to become the President of the later Coordinating Council for the Measures aimed at the Prevention and Control of Underage Criminality.

[54] See note 18.

[55] United Nations Archives and Records Management Section. Fonds International Penal and Penitentiary Commission (1872–1955) - AG-010, S-0915-0002-0003-00001-UC, IPCC Délégation de la Grèce, 1946–1950, Correspondance.

ber states were appointed consultant experts at the United Nations. It seems that Greece started to participate again as member of the UN Commission for the Prevention of Crime and the Treatment of Offenders after this last development—that came after the end of the Civil War—which also excused the authorities from the annual subscription. This participation became more visible and substantial during the 1960s, as both official representatives and individual participants regularly took part in the United Nations conferences on the issue, while the Juvenile Department of the Ministry of Justice provided information to the surveys on juvenile delinquency undertaken by the Council of Europe.[56]

However, studying the material deposited, discussed, and processed by these international bodies concerning the efforts undertaken in Greece to contain and prevent juvenile delinquency, it is difficult for the researcher to recognise the consistently embellished image that it conveys. A number of examples can illustrate this point.

First, it is not possible to verify the data that the Greek authorities provided to the international organizations regarding the extent of juvenile delinquency in the country. While it was repeatedly stated that Greece contributed data from 1951, there is nothing to corroborate this assumption, since the post-war official penal and criminological statistics were not published prior to 1957. However, claiming this unverifiable data, the Greek authorities stated in their contribution to the 1962 survey for the European Committee on Crime Problems of the Council that, although the Greek programmes of prevention were as yet rudimentary, juvenile crime remained low

---

[56] See notes 20 and 29.

"as much in respect to the number of delinquent youth as in respect to the nature of their antisocial behaviour and the offences that they committed."[57] While juvenile delinquency was a national concern at home, claiming its low levels became a matter of national pride abroad.

Second, in all the reports, the same data were used in the comparisons between different countries as to the extent of juvenile delinquency. Greece was presented among the European countries which showed "a slow but fairly steady increase in juvenile delinquency," but a lesser one than elsewhere. This was attributed to the fact that the country was listed among those "where there was a lesser degree of industrialization but perhaps greater emphasis on family ties."[58] Correlating the new forms of juvenile delinquency with social, economic, and cultural conditions in the various countries, the experts of the international organizations piled one unsubstantiated interpretation upon another by resorting to widespread hierarchical stereotypes regarding the effects of economic organization on social relations.

Third, Greek authorities repeatedly claimed shortage of funds as an excuse for various inefficiencies: the lack of systematic research into methods of prevention, the non-existence of large-scale preventive action, the non-implementation of the measures proposed by the Council for the Co-ordination of Juvenile Crime Prevention, and so forth. Bad finances were systematically linked to what was called "recent history," that is the bloody 1940s and their consequences—a very recent history indeed if we consider that the Civil War only ended in late 1949.

---

[57] ECCP 1963, pp. 37–43.
[58] See also ECCR 1960, p. 23; UN, *Juvenile Delinquency*, 1960, p. 9.

In an international or supranational context, Greek authorities presented these financial difficulties as the price that the country had to pay in order to remain in the midst of the "family of civilized nations." The argument did not pass unnoticed, especially by the Council of Europe, a body aligned to the Cold-War politics. As the writer of the 1962 survey report noted: "the account of prevention in Greece might well have been presented under the title of 'Putting First Things First'": it was realistically geared to "particular conditions, recent history and current resources." Therefore, "formal scientific evaluation of preventive measures may have to take second place."[59] However, as we saw, it was as much shortage of funds as the dominant moral perspective on juvenile delinquency that determined the way juvenile delinquency was addressed at home.

Fourth, the workings of the Council for the Coordination of Juvenile Crime Prevention were systematically exaggerated: it was routinely given more importance in the reports than it actually had: not only was this the only coordinating initiative by the authorities, but also none of the measures that it proposed were adopted. Everything indicates that the Greek authorities were more interested in presenting a positive image of the country in these international fora, irrespective of the actual situation, than in drawing from the experiences of others and forging collaborations. They seemed even less prepared to accept the prevailing new approaches that substituted penal with "psy" expertise.[60]

---

[59] ECCP 1963, pp. 42–43.

[60] The constant reproduction by the Greek authorities of the existing scant information long after it became outdated often led to misunderstandings and misinterpretations when handled by international

Finally, the profile of the Greek participants in the successive UN conferences enhances this contention, to the extent that the existing material from the successive UN conferences on the issue provides names: both government representatives and individual participants were all jurists, lawyers, or senior civil servants of the Ministry of Justice. No other Greek professional group was ever represented on these occasions. This corroborates the argument that scientific expertise on matters related to juvenile delinquency and its prevention, which flourished by then in other countries, had as yet no public leverage in Greece, where the issue remained in the hands of jurists.[61] At the same time, all participants were members of a wide and diverse network of an "acting elite of doers,"[62] individuals alternating between official and unofficial positions, the privileged interlocutors to the ministries and state services responsible for juvenile delinquency or in fact on any matter pertaining to

---

officials unfamiliar with the Greek situation. Take for example the way juvenile probation was presented in the UNESCO report on juvenile delinquency as a problem of the modern world, published by the American professor of the University of Boston, William C. Kvaraceus, in 1964 (Kvaraceus, *La Délinquance juvénile, problème du monde modern*). Eight years after juvenile probation officers became the paid staff of the Greek Juvenile Probation Office, the writer maintained that juvenile probation was in Greece a voluntary mission. Even more, he contended that the lack of a suitable office to house probation officers had the positive consequence that it obliged them to visit the minors at home! Needless to say, this was the usual practice for the juvenile probation officers who either prepared the report of social investigation for the juvenile judge or regularly followed-up the minors in their responsibility.

[61] Avdela, "Youth 'in Moral Danger'".

[62] To borrow the term proposed by P. Becker and J. H. Dekker, "Doers: The Emergence of an Acting Elite", *Paedagogica Historica: International Journal of the History of Education* 38/2-3, 2002, pp. 427–432.

vulnerable groups. However, they were yet far from becoming part of the so-called "Third UN."[63]

Traditional approaches and national pride were not the only motives for the way Greek authorities operated in the international fora that were preoccupied with the issue of juvenile delinquency. In the post-Civil-War conditions of "scrubby democracy,"[64] it seems that what was important to the authorities in order to ensure international (Western) legitimacy was more the very fact of participating in these—and other—international bodies than the need to organize interventions or gain knowledge and experience. The embellished picture of the initiatives and measures undertaken for the prevention and containment of juvenile delinquency was part of this policy of international "public relations."

In fact, we may wonder whether they did more or less the same as the representatives of other countries: they considered it their national duty to present abroad a "nice image" of their country. Because, despite the particular circumstances in each case, in Greece as elsewhere the public concerns about juvenile delinquency in that period were in fact one of the ways through which post-war societies and their governments were convinced that the proper conduct of their youth (however this proper conduct was conceived and however difficult it was to

---

63 Jolly, Emmerij, Weiss, *UN Ideas That Changed the World*, pp. 32–33. They termed 'Third UN' "the NGOs, academics, consultants, experts, independent commissions, and other groups of individuals who routinely engage with the First UN [member states] and the Second UN [staff members] and thereby influence UN thinking, policies, priorities, and actions. The key characteristic for this third sphere is its independence from governments and UN secretaries", p. 33.

64 I. Nikolakopoulos, *Η καχεκτική δημοκρατία. Κόμματα και εκλογές, 1946–1967* [*Scrubby Democracy. Parties and Elections, 1946–1967*], Athens, 2001.

ensure) was a necessary indicator of social order and progress in the prevailing conditions of dramatic change.

Conclusion

In the 1960 publication of the 1958 survey of the European Committee on Crime Problems on "Some aspects of post-war juvenile delinquency" in twelve of the member countries of the Council of Europe, Lodovico Benvenuti, the Council's Italian secretary general from 1957 to 1964, wrote in the foreword:

> The problem of juvenile delinquency cannot be considered apart from that of youth in general; and the latter problem arises with increasing urgency in a society faced with constant and difficult changes. It is a problem of the future; and Europe has become too conscious of its past to afford to neglect its future.[65]

A former partisan, an experienced politician and an ardent defender of European unification, Benvenuti had a clear measure of the political dimension of juvenile delinquency in the post-war years. However, it would take almost a decade for European politicians and opinion makers to leave the question of juvenile delinquency to the various experts and concentrate on "youth." By then new anxieties emerged of different content and form. They concerned the youth movement, with its culture and its political radicalization. These were considered more a matter of policies than of justice and morality.

As the public concerns about juvenile delinquency subsided all over Europe in the mid-1960s the issue ceased

---

[65] ECCP 1960, p. 3.

also to be a priority for the international organizations mentioned above. It remained peripheral in the quinquennial United Nations crime congresses and it was seldom brought up by the Council of Europe.[66] Compared with developments in psychology, psychiatry, and social sciences and the growing critique of juridical mechanisms in all their aspects, juvenile delinquency was increasingly seen as a matter of education rather than one of punishment.[67]

In Greece also, until the military coup of 1967, the issue was slowly and gradually depoliticized, in the sense of turning into a matter of administrative, juridical, and social rather than political concern, even if the dictatorial regime of 1967–1974 was greatly concerned about the influences of the "global '68" on Greek youth. At any rate, "strayed" youth remained for much longer the prerogative of jurists and juvenile probation officers; psychologists and psychiatrists had great difficulty until the late seventies in having their opinion taken into account.[68] Moralism also remained dominant until the reestablishment of democratic institutions in 1974 and the rapid political, economic, and social changes of the seventies. By then, experts as well as opinion makers had

---

[66] United Nations Office for Drugs and Crime (UNODC), *United Nations Congresses on Crime Prevention and Criminal Justice 1955–2010. 55 Years of Achievement*, United Nations Information Service, Austria, 2010; Council of Europe—Committee of Ministers, *Recommendation No. R (87) 20 of the Committee of Ministers to Member States on Social Reactions to Juvenile Delinquency, 1987*, CE-CM-recR(87)20e-1987, Bibliotèque Nationale, Paris.

[67] For this evolution in the case of France, see V. Blanchard and M. Gardet, *Mauvaise graine. Deux siècles d'histoire de la justice des enfants*, Paris, 2017, pp. 143–157. For the reversal of this progressive turn by the end of the twentieth century, see J. Muncie, "The 'Punitive Turn' in Juvenile Justice: Cultures of Control and Rights Compliance in Western Europe and the USA", *Youth Justice* 8/2, 2008, pp. 107–121.

[68] Avdela, "Youth 'in Moral Danger'", *op. cit.*, 87–90.

ceased to talk about "underage criminality" and accepted the use of the term "juvenile delinquency" for the unlawful behavior of minors, while "moral danger" was abolished as a cause for the intervention of the juvenile justice mechanism. As Dr. T. S. Gibbens had maintained already in 1961, it became all the more obvious that juvenile delinquency was the product of severe deprivation and of serious disruption of social relations, and as such it constantly changed its form.

Sources

Unpublished

Kiriakopoulos, A., Alternative General Secretary of the National Federation of Greek Unions, speech in the auditorium of the Federation for the "Week of the Neglected Child" in 1958, mimeo, Archives of Union History, NFGU.

United Nations Archives and Records Management Section. Fonds International Penal and Penitentiary Commission (1872–1955) - AG-010, S-0915-0068-0005-00001 Part A UC: IPU, XXIIe Congrès pénal et pénitentiaire international de Rome, 1940; 1) Rapport présenté par M. Andreas Ch. Christodoulou, Directeur de l'Ecole d'éducation surveillée de Syros, Grèce; 2) Rapport présenté par M. le Dr. Themistocle G. Papaefstathiou, Directeur en chef de l'administration pénitentiaire, Athènes; 3) Rapport de M. G. Katopodis, Directeur de la prison-école 'Averoff' et de la Prison centrale des femmes (Athènes).

United Nations Archives and Records Management Section. Fonds International Penal and Penitentiary Commission (1872–1955) - AG-010, S-0915-0002-0003-00001-UC, IPCC Délégation de la Grèce, 1946–1950, Correspondance.

World Health Organization, *New Forms of Juvenile Delinquency; Their Origin, Prevention and Treatment*, Report from the World Health Organization to the Second United Nations Congress on the Prevention of Crime and the Treatment of Offenders, typed, LSE Library, London, 1960.

Published

Bovet, L., *Psychiatric Aspects of Juvenile Delinquency*, World Health Organization, Palais des Nations, Geneva, 1951.

Commission internationale de police criminelle, *La Délinquance juvénile actuelle, ses formes et ses causes, ainsi que les mesures propres à sa prévention dans le cadre de la lutte internationale contre la criminalité. XVIe session, Paris, 9–12 June 1947. N° 15, Rapport du Dr M. Sebor*, Paris, 1947.

Council of Europe–Committee of Ministers, *Recommendation No. R (87) 20 of the Committee of Ministers to Member States on Social Reactions to Juvenile Delinquency, 1987*, CE-CM-recR(87)20e-1987, Bibliotèque Nationale, Paris.

European Committee on Crime Problems, *Juvenile Delinquency in Post-War Europe*, Council of Europe, Strasburg, 1960.

European Committee on Crime Problems, *The Effectiveness of Current Programmes for the Prevention of Juvenile Delinquency*, Council of Europe, Strasburg, 1963.

Gibbens, T. C., *New Forms of Juvenile Delinquency; Their Origin, Prevention and Treatment*, World Health Organization, Geneva, 1961.

Kvaraceus, William C., *La Délinquance juvénile, problème du monde moderne*, UNESCO, Paris, 1964.

Ministry of Justice, General Direction of Penal Justice, Direction of Administration and General Inspection, Section of Minors, *Σκοποί—προσπάθειαι—επιτεύξεις Συμβουλίου συντονισμού των μέτρων διά τους ανηλίκους. Στατιστική έρευνα της εγκληματικότητος. Διεθνείς υποδείξεις, Έκθεσις Γ. Απ. Κατωπόδη, Διευθυντού Διοικήσεως και Γενικής Επιθεωρήσεως Φυλακών και*

Καταστημάτων Ανηλίκων, υποβληθείσα προς τον Κον Υπουργόν της Δικαιοσύνης [*Aims–Efforts–Achievements of the Council Coordinating the Measures for Minors. International Suggestions. Report by G. A. Katopodis, Director of Administration and General Inspection of Prisons and Institutions for Minors, submitted to the Minister of Justice*], Athens, 1956.

Official Minutes of the Parliamentary Sessions, 12 December 1952–10 June 1953, Athens, 1953, pp. 280–284 (in Greek).

Organisation des Nations Unies, *La Probation (Régime de la mise à l'épreuve) et les mesures analogue*, Melen, 1953.

United Nations, Department of Economic and Social Affairs, *Second United Nations Congress for the Prevention of Crime and the Treatment of Delinquents*, London, 1960. Special Police Departments for the Prevention of Juvenile Delinquency, Submitted by the International Criminal Police Organization—INTERPOL, General Secretariat, Paris, 1960.

United Nations, Department of Economic and Social Affairs, *Second United Nation Congress on the Prevention of Crime, UN Reports, New Forms of Juvenile Delinquency: Their Origin, Prevention and Treatment*, Paris, 1960.

United Nations, Department of Economic and Social Affairs, *Third United Nations Congress on the Prevention of Crime and the Treatment of Offenders*, Stockholm, 9–18 August 1965, New York, 1967.

United Nations Office for Drugs and Crime (UNODC), *United Nations Congresses on Crime Prevention and Criminal Justice 1955–2010. 55 Years of Achievement*, United Nations Information Service, Austria, 2010.

Bibliography

Ajzenstadt, M., "Reactions to Juvenile Delinquency in Israel, 1950–1970: A Social Narrative", *The Journal of Policy History* 17/4, 2005, pp. 404–425.

Avdela, E., "'Corrupting and Uncontrollable Activities': Moral Panic about Youth in Post-Civil-War Greece", *Journal of Contemporary History* 43/1, 2008, pp. 25–44.

Avdela, E., *"Νέοι εν κινδύνω." Επιτήρηση, αναμόρφωση και δικαιοσύνη ανηλίκων μετά τον πόλεμο* [*"Youth in Danger." Surveillance, Reformation and Juvenile Justice after the War*], Athens, 2013.

Avdela E., "Between Voluntary Workers and Public Servants: Juvenile Probation Officers in Greece, 1954–1976", in Ada Dialla andNiki Maroniti (eds), *State, Economy, Society (19th–20th centuries). Essays in Honor of Emeritus Professor George B. Dertilis*, Athens, 2013, pp. 27–53.

Avdela, E., "Growing up in the 'Dangerous' Neighborhoods of Post-war Thessaloniki", in Evangelia Tressou, Soula Mitakidou, Giota Karagianni (eds), *Roma Inclusion, International and Greek Experiences. Complexities of Inclusion*, Thessalonki, 2015, pp. 179–186.

Avdela, E., "Youth 'in Moral Danger': (Re)conceptualizing Delinquency in Post-Civil-War Greece", *Social History* 42/1, 2017, pp. 73–93.

Avdela E. and Vassiliadou, Dimitra, "'Sauver l'enfant dévoyé' : La Société pour la protection des mineurs d'Athènes après la guerre", *Revue d'histoire de l'enfance 'irrégulière'* 18, 2016, 299–317.

Becker, P. and Dekker, J. H., "Doers: The Emergence of an Acting Elite", *Paedagogica Historica: International Journal of the History of Education* 38/2-3, 2002, pp. 427–432.

Bertrams, K., and Kott, S., "Actions sociales transnationales", *Genèses* 71/2, 2008, pp. 2–3.

Binder, A., Geis, A., and Bruce, D. D., *Juvenile Delinquency. Historical, Cultural, Legal Perspectives*, Cincinnati, 1997.

Blanchard, V., and Gardet, M., *Mauvaise graine. Deux siècles d'histoire de la justice des enfants*, Paris, 2017.

Bradley, K., Logan, A., and Shaw, S., "Editorial: Youth and Crime: Centennial Reflections on the Children Act 1908", *Crimes and Misdemeanours* 3/2, 2009, p. 1–17.

Close, D. H., *The Origins of the Greek Civil War*, London, 1993.

Cohen, S., *Folk Devils and Moral Panics: The Creation of the Mods and Rockers*, London, 1972.

Dupont-Bouchat, M.-S., "Du tourisme pénitentiaire à 'l'Internationale des philanthropes'. La création d'un réseau pour la protection de l'enfance à travers les congrès internationaux (1840–1914)", *Paedagogica Historica: International Journal of the History of Education* 38/2-3, 2002, pp. 533–563.

Droux, J., "L'internationalisation de la protection de l'enfance : acteurs, concurrences et projets transnationaux (1900–1925) ", *Critique internationale* 52/3, 2011, pp. 17–33.

Edele, M., "Strange Young Men in Stalin's Moscow: The Birth and Life of the Stiliagi, 1945–1953", *Jahrbücher für Geschichte Osteuropas* 50/1, 2002, pp. 37–61.

Ellis, H., "Editor's Introduction: Juvenile Delinquency, Modernity, and the State", *Social Justice* 38/4, 2011, pp. 1–10.

Ellis, H., (ed.), *Juvenile Delinquency and the Limits of Western Influence, 1850–2000*, London, 2014.

Fürst, J., *Stalin's Last Generation. Soviet Post-War Youth and the Emergence of Mature Socialism*, Oxford, 2010.

Gilbert, J., *A Cycle of Outrage. America's Reaction to the Juvenile Delinquent in the 1950s*, Oxford, 1986.

Haas, P., "Introduction: Epistemic Communities and International Policy", *International Organization* 46/1, 1992, pp. 1–35.

Horn, G.-R., *The Spirit of '68: Rebellion in Western Europe and North America, 1956–1976*, Oxford, 2007.

Horváth, S., "Patchwork Identities and Folk Devils: Youth Subcultures and Gangs in Socialist Hungary", *Social History* 34/2, 2009, pp. 163–183.

Iriye, A., *Global Community. The Role of International Organizations in the Making of the Contemporary World*, Los Angeles, London, 2002.

Iriye, A., (ed.), *Global Interdependence. The World after 1945*, Cambridge, Mass., London, 2014.

Jackson, L., with A. Bartie, *Policing Youth: Britain 1945–70*, Manchester, 2014.

Jarvis, M., *Conservative Governments, Morality and Social Change in Affluent Britain, 1957–64*, Manchester, 2005.

Jolly, R., Emmerij, L., and Weiss, T. G., *UN Ideas that Changed the World*, Bloomington & Indianapolis, 2009.

Komen, M., "Dangerous Children: Juvenile Delinquency and Judicial Intervention in the Netherlands, 1960–1995", *Crime, Law & Social Change* 37, 2002, pp. 379–401.

Kott, S., "Une 'communauté épistémique' du social ? Experts de l'OIT et internationalisation des politiques sociales dans l'entre-deux-guerres", *Genèses* 71/2, 2008, pp. 26–46.

Leonards, C., "Border Crossings: Care and the 'Criminal Child' in Nineteenth Century European Penal Congresses", in P. Cox and H. Shore (eds), *Becoming Delinquent: European Youth, 1650–1950*, Aldershot, 2002, pp. 105–121.

Lopez-Rey, M., "The First U. N. Congress on the Prevention of Crime and the Treatment of Offenders", *Journal of Criminal Law and Criminology* 47/5, 1957, pp. 526–538.

Mazower, M., *No Enchanted Palace. The End of Empire and the Ideological Origins of the United Nations*, Princeton, 2009.

Muncie, J., *Youth and Crime. A Critical Introduction*, London, 1999.

Muncie, J., "The 'Punitive Turn' in Juvenile Justice: Cultures of Control and Rights Compliance in Western Europe and the USA", *Youth Justice* 8/2, 2008, pp. 107–121.

Muncie, J. and Hughes, G., "Modes of Youth Governance. Political Rationalities, Criminalization and Resistance", in J. Muncie, G. Hughes, and E. McLaughlin (eds), *Youth Justice. Critical Readings*, London–New Delhi, 2002, pp. 1–18.

Nikolakopoulos, I., *Η καχεκτική δημοκρατία. Κόμματα και εκλογές, 1946–1967* [*Scrubby democracy. Parties and elections, 1946–1967*], Athens, 2001.

Nilsson, R., "Creating the Swedish Juvenile Delinquent: Criminal Policy, Science and Institutionalization c. 1930–1970", *Scandinavian Journal of History* 34/4, 2009, pp. 354–375.

Papagerakis, I. P., *Οι μεταπολεμικοί ανήλικοι (Μελέτη κοινωνιολογική, ψυχολογική και παιδαγωγική)* [*Post-war Minors (A Sociological, Psychological and Pedagogic Study)*], Thessaloniki, 1956.

Passerini, L., "La jeunesse comme métaphore du changement social. Deux débats sur les jeunes: L'Italie fasciste, l'Amérique des années 1950", in G. Levi and J.-C. Schmitt (eds), *Histoire des jeunes en Occident*, vol. 2: *L'époque contemporaine* Paris, 1996, pp. 339–408.

Petrakis, M., *The Metaxas Myth: Dictatorship and Propaganda in Greece*, London, 2006.

Piccone Stella, S., "'Rebels without a Cause': Male Youth in Italy around 1960", *History Workshop Journal* 38, 1994, pp. 157–178.

Rose, N., *Governing the Soul. The Shaping of the Private Self*, London–New York, 1999.

Sayward, A. L., *The United Nations in International History*, London, Oxford, 2017).

Sfikas, T. D. and Carabott, P., (eds), *The Greek Civil War. Essays on a Conflict of Exceptionalism and Silences*, Aldershot, 2004.

Theodorou, V. and Vassiloudi, V., "'Για να σφυρηλατήσουμε καλύτερους και πιο υπεύθυνους χαρακτήρες": Ψυχολογικά εργαλεία ηθικοποίησης της νεότητας στη μετεμφυλιακή Ελλάδα' [*'In order to forge better and more responsible characters': Psychological tools for the moralisation of youth in post-Civil-War Greece*], paper delivered at the Fourteenth Panhellenic Congress of Psychological Research, Alexandroupoli, 15–19 May 2013.

Wassenberg, B., *History of the Council of Europe*, Strasburg, 2013.

Wills, A., "Delinquency, Masculinity and Citizenship in England 1950–1970", *Past & Present* 187, 2005, pp. 157–185.

Zahra, T., *The Lost Children. Reconstructing Europe's Families after World War II*, Harvard, 2015.

Gunnar Hering Lectures

The books are based on yearly lectures that take place in spring at the Department of Byzantine and Modern Greek Studies of the University of Vienna. Both the lectures program and the book series are named after the first professor of the Chair of Modern Greek Studies, Gunnar Hering. The authors are leading scholars in European and Southeast European history.

Lecture 2016

Dimitris Stamatopoulos
The Eastern Question or Balkan Nationalism(s)
Balkan History Reconsidered

Gunnar Hering Lectures, Vol. 1
2018, 64 pages, paperback
€ 13,– D / € 14,– A
ISBN 978-3-8471-0830-6
Vienna University Press by V&R unipress

Open Access:
www.vandenhoeck-ruprecht-verlage.com

Lecture 2018

François Hartog
„Die schönste Erfindung der Neuzeit"
Das antike Griechenland in der Vorstellung Europas

Vandenhoeck & Ruprecht Verlage

 unipress   www.vandenhoeck-ruprecht-verlage.com